Statutory framework for the early years foundation stage

Setting the standards for learning, development and care for children from birth to five

Published: 3 March 2017

Effective: 3 April 2017

Contents

Summary

About this statutory framework

This framework is mandatory for all early years providers in England (from 3 April 2017)[1]: maintained schools; non-maintained schools; independent schools; all providers on the Early Years Register; and all providers registered with an early years childminder agency[2].

Ofsted and inspectorates of independent schools have regard to the Early Years Foundation Stage (EYFS) in carrying out inspections and report on the quality and standards of provision. Ofsted publishes inspection reports at www.gov.uk/ofsted. Ofsted may issue actions (in respect of any failure to meet a requirement in the document) and/or may issue a welfare requirements notice (in respect of Section 3). It is an offence for a provider to fail to comply with a welfare requirements notice. Early years childminder agencies are also under a duty to have regard to the EYFS in the exercise of their functions.

The learning and development requirements in sections 1 and 2 of this framework, and the safeguarding and welfare requirements in section 3 of this framework, are indicated by the use of the word "must". Additionally, early years providers must "have regard" to other provisions in these sections. These provisions are indicated by the use of the word "should". "Having regard" to these provisions means that early years providers must take them into account when providing early years provision and should not depart from them unless there is good reason for doing so.

Expiry or review date

This statutory framework remains in force until further notice.

What legislation does this framework refer to?

- The learning and development requirements are given legal force by an Order[3] made under section 39(1)(a) of the Childcare Act 2006

- The safeguarding and welfare requirements are given legal force by Regulations[4] made under section 39(1)(b) of the Childcare Act 2006

---

[1] Section 46 of the Childcare Act 2006 enables the Secretary of State to confer exemptions from the learning and development requirements in certain prescribed circumstances.
[2] The Childcare (Exemptions from Registration) Order 2008 (S.I.2008/979) specifies the circumstances in which providers are not required to register.
[3] The Early Years Foundation Stage (Learning and Development Requirements) Order 2007 (S.I. 2007/1772), as amended.
[4] The Early Years Foundation Stage (Welfare Requirements) Regulations 2012 (S.I. 2012/938), as amended.

Who is this framework for?

This framework is for all early years providers in England (from 3 April 2017): maintained schools; non-maintained schools; independent schools (including free schools and academies); all providers on the Early Years Register; and all providers registered with an early years childminder agency (CMA).

Introduction

1. Every child deserves the best possible start in life and the support that enables them to fulfil their potential. Children develop quickly in the early years and a child's experiences between birth and age five have a major impact on their future life chances. A secure, safe and happy childhood is important in its own right. Good parenting and high quality early learning together provide the foundation children need to make the most of their abilities and talents as they grow up.

2. The Early Years Foundation Stage (EYFS) sets the standards that all early years providers must meet to ensure that children learn and develop well and are kept healthy and safe. It promotes teaching and learning to ensure children's 'school readiness' and gives children the broad range of knowledge and skills that provide the right foundation for good future progress through school and life.

3. The EYFS seeks to provide:

   - **quality and consistency** in all early years settings, so that every child makes good progress and no child gets left behind

   - **a secure foundation** through learning and development opportunities which are planned around the needs and interests of each individual child and are assessed and reviewed regularly

   - **partnership working** between practitioners and with parents and/or carers

   - **equality of opportunity** and anti-discriminatory practice, ensuring that every child is included and supported

4. The EYFS specifies requirements for learning and development and for safeguarding children and promoting their welfare. The **learning and development requirements** cover:

   - the **areas of learning and development** which must shape activities and experiences (**educational programmes**) for children in all early years settings

   - the **early learning goals** that providers must help children work towards (the knowledge, skills and understanding children should have at the end of the academic year in which they turn five)

   - **assessment arrangements** for measuring progress (and requirements for reporting to parents and/or carers)

5. The **safeguarding and welfare requirements** cover the steps that providers must take to keep children safe and promote their welfare.

Overarching principles

6. Four guiding principles should shape practice in early years settings. These are:

    - every child is a **unique child**, who is constantly learning and can be resilient, capable, confident and self-assured

    - children learn to be strong and independent through **positive relationships**

    - children learn and develop well in **enabling environments**, in which their experiences respond to their individual needs and there is a strong partnership between practitioners and parents and/or carers

    - **children develop and learn in different ways** (see "the characteristics of effective teaching and learning" at paragraph 1.9) **and at different rates**. The framework covers the education and care of all children in early years provision, including children with special educational needs and disabilities.

Section 1 – The learning and development requirements

1.1. This section defines what providers[5] must do, working in partnership with parents and/or carers, to promote the learning and development of all children in their care, and to ensure they are ready for school. The learning and development requirements are informed by the best available evidence on how children learn and reflect the broad range of skills, knowledge and attitudes children need as foundations for good future progress. Early years providers must guide the development of children's capabilities with a view to ensuring that children in their care complete the EYFS ready to benefit fully from the opportunities ahead of them.

1.2. The EYFS learning and development requirements comprise:

- the seven areas of learning and development and the educational programmes (described below)

- the early learning goals, which summarise the knowledge, skills and understanding that all young children should have gained by the end of the Reception year

- the assessment requirements (when and how practitioners must assess children's achievements, and when and how they should discuss children's progress with parents and/or carers)

The areas of learning and development

1.3. There are seven areas of learning and development that must shape educational programmes in early years settings. All areas of learning and development are important and inter-connected. Three areas are particularly crucial for igniting children's curiosity and enthusiasm for learning, and for building their capacity to learn, form relationships and thrive. These three areas, the prime areas, are:

- communication and language

- physical development

- personal, social and emotional development

---

[5] Providers offering care exclusively before and after school or during the school holidays for children who normally attend Reception (or older) class during the school day (see paragraph 3.40) do not need to meet the learning and development requirements. However, providers offering care exclusively before and after school or during the school holidays for children younger than those in the Reception class age range, should continue to be guided by, but do not have to meet, the learning and development requirements. All such providers should discuss with parents and/or carers (and other practitioners/providers as appropriate, including school staff/teachers) the support they intend to offer.

1.4. Providers must also support children in four specific areas, through which the three prime areas are strengthened and applied. The specific areas are:

- literacy
- mathematics
- understanding the world
- expressive arts and design

1.5. Educational programmes must involve activities and experiences for children, as follows:

- **Communication and language** development involves giving children opportunities to experience a rich language environment; to develop their confidence and skills in expressing themselves; and to speak and listen in a range of situations

- **Physical development** involves providing opportunities for young children to be active and interactive; and to develop their co-ordination, control, and movement. Children must also be helped to understand the importance of physical activity[6], and to make healthy choices in relation to food

- **Personal, social and emotional development** involves helping children to develop a positive sense of themselves, and others; to form positive relationships and develop respect for others; to develop social skills and learn how to manage their feelings; to understand appropriate behaviour in groups; and to have confidence in their own abilities

- **Literacy** development involves encouraging children to link sounds and letters and to begin to read and write. Children must be given access to a wide range of reading materials (books, poems, and other written materials) to ignite their interest

- **Mathematics** involves providing children with opportunities to develop and improve their skills in counting, understanding and using numbers, calculating simple addition and subtraction problems; and to describe shapes, spaces, and measure

- **Understanding the world** involves guiding children to make sense of their physical world and their community through opportunities to explore, observe and find out about people, places, technology and the environment

- **Expressive arts and design** involves enabling children to explore and play with a wide range of media and materials, as well as providing opportunities and encouragement for sharing their thoughts, ideas and feelings through a

---

[6] The Chief Medical Office has published guidance on physical activity that providers may wish to refer to, which is available at: www.gov.uk/government/publications/uk-physical-activity-guidelines.

variety of activities in art, music, movement, dance, role-play, and design and technology

1.6. Practitioners must consider the individual needs, interests, and stage of development of each child in their care, and must use this information to plan a challenging and enjoyable experience for each child in all of the areas of learning and development. Practitioners working with the youngest children are expected to focus strongly on the three prime areas, which are the basis for successful learning in the other four specific areas. The three prime areas reflect the key skills and capacities all children need to develop and learn effectively, and become ready for school. It is expected that the balance will shift towards a more equal focus on all areas of learning as children grow in confidence and ability within the three prime areas. But throughout the early years, if a child's progress in any prime area gives cause for concern, practitioners must discuss this with the child's parents and/or carers and agree how to support the child. Practitioners must consider whether a child may have a special educational need or disability which requires specialist support. They should link with, and help families to access, relevant services from other agencies as appropriate.

1.7. For children whose home language is not English, providers must take reasonable steps to provide opportunities for children to develop and use their home language in play and learning, supporting their language development at home. Providers must also ensure that children have sufficient opportunities to learn and reach a good standard in English language during the EYFS: ensuring children are ready to benefit from the opportunities available to them when they begin Year 1. When assessing communication, language and literacy skills, practitioners must assess children's skills in English. If a child does not have a strong grasp of English language, practitioners must explore the child's skills in the home language with parents and/or carers, to establish whether there is cause for concern about language delay.

1.8. Each area of learning and development must be implemented through planned, purposeful play and through a mix of adult-led and child-initiated activity. Play is essential for children's development, building their confidence as they learn to explore, to think about problems, and relate to others. Children learn by leading their own play, and by taking part in play which is guided by adults. There is an ongoing judgement to be made by practitioners about the balance between activities led by children, and activities led or guided by adults. Practitioners must respond to each child's emerging needs and interests, guiding their development through warm, positive interaction. As children grow older, and as their development allows, it is expected that the balance will gradually shift towards more activities led by adults, to help children prepare for more formal learning, ready for Year 1.

1.9. In planning and guiding children's activities, practitioners must reflect on the different ways that children learn and reflect these in their practice. Three characteristics of effective teaching and learning are:

- **playing and exploring** - children investigate and experience things, and 'have a go'

- **active learning** - children concentrate and keep on trying if they encounter difficulties, and enjoy achievements

- **creating and thinking critically** - children have and develop their own ideas, make links between ideas, and develop strategies for doing things

1.10. Each child must be assigned a key person[7] (also a safeguarding and welfare requirement - see paragraph 3.27). Providers must inform parents and/or carers of the name of the key person, and explain their role, when a child starts attending a setting. The key person must help ensure that every child's learning and care is tailored to meet their individual needs. The key person must seek to engage and support parents and/or carers in guiding their child's development at home. They should also help families engage with more specialist support if appropriate.

1.11. A quality learning experience for children requires a quality workforce. A well-qualified, skilled staff strongly increases the potential of any individual setting to deliver the best possible outcomes for children. Requirements in relation to staff qualifications are outlined in Section 3.

1.12. The level of progress children should be expected to have attained by the end of the EYFS is defined by the early learning goals set out below.

The early learning goals

The prime areas

Communication and language

Listening and attention: children listen attentively in a range of situations. They listen to stories, accurately anticipating key events and respond to what they hear with relevant comments, questions or actions. They give their attention to what others say and respond appropriately, while engaged in another activity.

Understanding: children follow instructions involving several ideas or actions. They answer 'how' and 'why' questions about their experiences and in response to stories or events.

Speaking: children express themselves effectively, showing awareness of listeners' needs. They use past, present and future forms accurately when talking about events

---

[7] In childminding settings, the key person is the childminder.

that have happened or are to happen in the future. They develop their own narratives and explanations by connecting ideas or events.

Physical development

Moving and handling: children show good control and co-ordination in large and small movements. They move confidently in a range of ways, safely negotiating space. They handle equipment and tools effectively, including pencils for writing.

Health and self-care: children know the importance for good health of physical exercise, and a healthy diet, and talk about ways to keep healthy and safe. They manage their own basic hygiene and personal needs successfully, including dressing and going to the toilet independently.

Personal, social and emotional development

Self-confidence and self-awareness: children are confident to try new activities, and say why they like some activities more than others. They are confident to speak in a familiar group, will talk about their ideas, and will choose the resources they need for their chosen activities. They say when they do or don't need help.

Managing feelings and behaviour: children talk about how they and others show feelings, talk about their own and others' behaviour, and its consequences, and know that some behaviour is unacceptable. They work as part of a group or class, and understand and follow the rules. They adjust their behaviour to different situations, and take changes of routine in their stride.

Making relationships: children play co-operatively, taking turns with others. They take account of one another's ideas about how to organise their activity. They show sensitivity to others' needs and feelings, and form positive relationships with adults and other children.

The specific areas

Literacy

Reading: children read and understand simple sentences. They use phonic knowledge to decode regular words and read them aloud accurately. They also read some common irregular words. They demonstrate understanding when talking with others about what they have read.

Writing: children use their phonic knowledge to write words in ways which match their spoken sounds. They also write some irregular common words. They write simple sentences which can be read by themselves and others. Some words are spelt correctly and others are phonetically plausible.

Mathematics

Numbers: children count reliably with numbers from 1 to 20, place them in order and say which number is one more or one less than a given number. Using quantities and objects, they add and subtract two single-digit numbers and count on or back to find the answer. They solve problems, including doubling, halving and sharing.

Shape, space and measures: children use everyday language to talk about size, weight, capacity, position, distance, time and money to compare quantities and objects and to solve problems. They recognise, create and describe patterns. They explore characteristics of everyday objects and shapes and use mathematical language to describe them.

Understanding the world

People and communities: children talk about past and present events in their own lives and in the lives of family members. They know that other children don't always enjoy the same things, and are sensitive to this. They know about similarities and differences between themselves and others, and among families, communities and traditions.

The world: children know about similarities and differences in relation to places, objects, materials and living things. They talk about the features of their own immediate environment and how environments might vary from one another. They make observations of animals and plants and explain why some things occur, and talk about changes.

Technology: children recognise that a range of technology is used in places such as homes and schools. They select and use technology for particular purposes.

Expressive arts and design

Exploring and using media and materials: children sing songs, make music and dance, and experiment with ways of changing them. They safely use and explore a variety of materials, tools and techniques, experimenting with colour, design, texture, form and function.

Being imaginative: children use what they have learnt about media and materials in original ways, thinking about uses and purposes. They represent their own ideas, thoughts and feelings through design and technology, art, music, dance, role-play and stories.

Section 2 – Assessment

2.1. Assessment plays an important part in helping parents, carers and practitioners to recognise children's progress, understand their needs, and to plan activities and support. Ongoing assessment (also known as formative assessment) is an integral part of the learning and development process. It involves practitioners observing children to understand their level of achievement, interests and learning styles, and to then shape learning experiences for each child reflecting those observations. In their interactions with children, practitioners should respond to their own day-to-day observations about children's progress and observations that parents and carers share.

2.2. Assessment should not entail prolonged breaks from interaction with children, nor require excessive paperwork. Paperwork should be limited to that which is absolutely necessary to promote children's successful learning and development. Parents and/or carers should be kept up-to-date with their child's progress and development. Practitioners should address any learning and development needs in partnership with parents and/or carers, and any relevant professionals.

Progress check at age two

2.3. When a child is aged between two and three, practitioners must review their progress, and provide parents and/or carers with a short written summary of their child's development in the prime areas. This progress check must identify the child's strengths, and any areas where the child's progress is less than expected. If there are significant emerging concerns, or an identified special educational need or disability, practitioners should develop a targeted plan to support the child's future learning and development involving parents and/or carers and other professionals (for example, the provider's Special Educational Needs Co-ordinator (SENCO) or health professionals) as appropriate.

2.4. Beyond the prime areas, it is for practitioners to decide what the written summary should include, reflecting the development level and needs of the individual child. The summary must highlight: areas in which a child is progressing well; areas in which some additional support might be needed; and focus particularly on any areas where there is a concern that a child may have a developmental delay (which may indicate a special educational need or disability). It must describe the activities and strategies the provider intends to adopt to address any issues or concerns. If a child moves settings between the ages of two and three it is expected that the progress check would usually be undertaken by the setting where the child has spent most time. Practitioners must discuss with parents and/or carers how the summary of development can be used to support learning at home.

2.5. Practitioners should encourage parents and/or carers to share information from the progress check with other relevant professionals, including their health visitor and the staff of any new provision the child may transfer to. Practitioners must agree with parents and/or carers when will be the most useful point to provide a summary. Where possible, the progress check and the Healthy Child Programme health and development review at age two (when health visitors gather information on a child's health and development) should inform each other and support integrated working. This will allow health and education professionals to identify strengths as well as any developmental delay and any particular support from which they think the child/family might benefit. Providers must have the consent of parents and/or carers to share information directly with other relevant professionals.

Assessment at the end of the EYFS – the Early Years Foundation Stage Profile (EYFSP)

2.6. In the final term of the year in which the child reaches age five, and no later than 30 June in that term, the EYFS Profile must be completed for each child. The Profile provides parents and carers, practitioners and teachers with a well-rounded picture of a child's knowledge, understanding and abilities, their progress against expected levels, and their readiness for Year 1. The Profile must reflect: ongoing observation; all relevant records held by the setting; discussions with parents and carers, and any other adults whom the teacher, parent or carer judges can offer a useful contribution.

2.7. Each child's level of development must be assessed against the early learning goals (see Section 1). Practitioners must indicate whether children are meeting expected levels of development, or if they are exceeding expected levels, or not yet reaching expected levels ('emerging'). This is the EYFS Profile.

2.8. Year 1 teachers must be given a copy of the Profile report together with a short commentary on each child's skills and abilities in relation to the three key characteristics of effective learning (see paragraph 1.9). These should inform a dialogue between Reception and Year 1 teachers about each child's stage of development and learning needs and assist with the planning of activities in Year 1.

2.9. Schools[8] must share the results of the Profile with parents and/or carers, and explain to them when and how they can discuss the Profile with the teacher[9] who completed it. For children attending more than one setting, the Profile must be completed by the school where the child spends most time. If a child moves to a new school during the academic year, the original school must send their assessment of the child's level of development against the early learning goals to

---

[8] Or the relevant provider.
[9] Or other practitioner.

the relevant school within 15 days of receiving a request. If a child moves during the summer term, relevant providers must agree which of them will complete the Profile.

2.10. The Profile must be completed for all children, including those with special educational needs or disabilities. Reasonable adjustments to the assessment process for children with special educational needs and disabilities must be made as appropriate. Providers should consider whether they may need to seek specialist assistance to help with this. Children will have differing levels of skills and abilities across the Profile and it is important that there is a full assessment of all areas of their development, to inform plans for future activities and to identify any additional support needs.

Information to be provided to the local authority

2.11. Early years providers must report EYFS Profile results to local authorities, upon request[10] Local authorities are under a duty to return this data to the relevant Government department. Providers must permit the relevant local authority to enter their premises to observe the completion of the EYFS Profile, and permit the relevant local authority to examine and take copies of documents and other articles relating to the Profile and assessments[11]. Providers must take part in all reasonable moderation activities specified by their local authority and provide the local authority with such information relating to the EYFS Profile and assessment as they may reasonably request.

---

[10] Childcare (Provision of Information about Young Children (England) Regulations 2009.
[11] The Early Years Foundation Stage (Learning and Development Requirements) Order 2007.

Section 3 – The safeguarding and welfare requirements

Introduction

3.1. Children learn best when they are healthy, safe and secure, when their individual needs are met, and when they have positive relationships with the adults caring for them. The safeguarding and welfare requirements, specified in this section, are designed to help providers create high quality settings which are welcoming, safe and stimulating, and where children are able to enjoy learning and grow in confidence.

3.2. Providers must take all necessary steps to keep children safe and well. The requirements in this section explain what early years providers must do to: safeguard children; ensure the suitability of adults who have contact with children; promote good health; manage behaviour; and maintain records, policies and procedures.

3.3. Schools are not required to have separate policies to cover EYFS requirements provided the requirements are already met through an existing policy. Where providers other than childminders are required to have policies and procedures as specified below, these policies and procedures should be recorded in writing. Childminders are not required to have written policies and procedures. However, they must be able to explain their policies and procedures to parents, carers, and others (for example Ofsted inspectors or the childminder agency with which they are registered) and ensure any assistants follow them.

Child protection

3.4. Providers must be alert to any issues of concern in the child's life at home or elsewhere. Providers must have and implement a policy, and procedures, to safeguard children. These should be in line with the guidance and procedures of the relevant Local Safeguarding Children Board (LSCB). The safeguarding policy and procedures must include an explanation of the action to be taken when there are safeguarding concerns about a child and in the event of an allegation being made against a member of staff, and cover the use of mobile phones and cameras in the setting.

3.5. A practitioner must be designated to take lead responsibility for safeguarding children in every setting. Childminders must take the lead responsibility themselves. The lead practitioner is responsible for liaison with local statutory children's services agencies, and with the LSCB. They must provide support, advice and guidance to any other staff on an ongoing basis, and on any specific safeguarding issue as required. The lead practitioner must attend a child protection training course[12] that enables them to identify, understand and respond appropriately to signs of possible abuse and neglect (as described at paragraph 3.6).

3.6. Providers must train all staff to understand their safeguarding policy and procedures, and ensure that all staff have up to date knowledge of safeguarding issues. Training made available by the provider must enable staff to identify signs of possible abuse and neglect at the earliest opportunity, and to respond in a timely and appropriate way. These may include:

- significant changes in children's behaviour

- deterioration in children's general well-being

- unexplained bruising, marks or signs of possible abuse or neglect

- children's comments which give cause for concern

- any reasons to suspect neglect or abuse outside the setting, for example in the child's home or that a girl may have been subjected to (or is at risk of) female genital mutilation[13] and/or

- inappropriate behaviour displayed by other members of staff, or any other person working with the children, for example: inappropriate sexual comments; excessive one-to-one attention beyond the requirements of their usual role and responsibilities; or inappropriate sharing of images

Providers may also find 'What to do if you're worried a child is being abused: Advice for practitioners'[14] helpful.

3.7. Providers must have regard to the government's statutory guidance 'Working Together to Safeguard Children 2015'[15] and to the 'Prevent duty guidance for England and Wales 2015'[16]. All schools are required to have regard[17] to the government's 'Keeping Children Safe in Education'[18] statutory guidance, and other childcare providers may also find it helpful to refer to this guidance. If providers have concerns about children's safety or welfare, they must notify agencies with statutory responsibilities without delay. This means the local children's social care services and, in emergencies, the police.

3.8. Registered providers must inform Ofsted or their childminder agency of any allegations of serious harm or abuse by any person living, working, or looking

---

[12] Taking account of any advice from the LSCB or local authority on appropriate training courses.

[13] www.gov.uk/government/publications/female-genital-mutilation-guidelines

[14] www.gov.uk/government/publications/what-to-do-if-youre-worried-a-child-is-being-abused--2

[15] www.gov.uk/government/uploads/system/uploads/attachment_data/file/419595/Working_Together_to _Safeguard_Children.pdf

[16] The 2015 Counter Terrorism and Security Act places a duty on early years providers "to have due regard to the need to prevent people from being drawn into terrorism" (the Prevent duty): www.gov.uk/government/publications/protecting-children-from-radicalisation-the-prevent-duty

[17] Under section 175(4) of the Education Act 2002

[18] www.gov.uk/government/publications/keeping-children-safe-in-education--2

after children at the premises (whether the allegations relate to harm or abuse committed on the premises or elsewhere). Registered providers must also notify Ofsted or their childminder agency of the action taken in respect of the allegations. These notifications must be made as soon as is reasonably practicable, but at the latest within 14 days of the allegations being made. A registered provider who, without reasonable excuse, fails to comply with this requirement, commits an offence.

Suitable people

3.9. Providers must ensure that people looking after children are suitable to fulfil the requirements of their roles. Providers must have effective systems in place to ensure that practitioners, and any other person who is likely to have regular contact with children (including those living or working on the premises), are suitable[19].

3.10. Ofsted or the agency with which the childminder is registered is responsible for checking the suitability of childminders, of every other person looking after children for whom the childminding is being provided (whether on domestic or non-domestic premises), and of every other person living or working on any domestic premises from which the childminding is being provided, including obtaining enhanced criminal records checks and barred list checks. Registered providers other than childminders must obtain an enhanced criminal records check in respect of every person aged 16 and over (including for unsupervised volunteers, and supervised volunteers who provide personal care[20]) who[21]:

- works directly with children

- lives on the premises on which the childcare is provided and/or

- works on the premises on which the childcare is provided (unless they do not work on the part of the premises where the childcare takes place, or do not work there at times when children are present)

An additional criminal records check (or checks if more than one country) should also be made for anyone who has lived or worked abroad[22].

---

[19] To allow Ofsted or the relevant childminder agency to make these checks, childminders are required to supply information to Ofsted or the relevant childminder agency, as set out in Schedule 1, Part 2 of the Childcare (Early Years Register) Regulations 2008, amended by the Childcare (Early Years Register) (Amendment) Regulations 2012. The requirements relating to people who live and work on childminder premises are in Schedule 1, Part 1.

[20] Personal care includes helping a child, for reasons of age, illness or disability, with eating or drinking, or in connection with toileting, washing, bathing and dressing.

[21] The requirement for a criminal records check will be deemed to have been met in respect of all people living or working in childcare settings, whose suitability was checked by Ofsted or their local authority before October 2005.

[22] See: www.gov.uk/government/publications/criminal-records-checks-for-overseas-applicants

3.11. Providers must tell staff that they are expected to disclose any convictions, cautions, court orders, reprimands and warnings[23] that may affect their suitability to work with children (whether received before or during their employment at the setting). Providers must not allow people, whose suitability has not been checked, including through a criminal records check[24], to have unsupervised contact with children being cared for.

3.12. Providers other than childminders must record information about staff qualifications and the identity checks and vetting processes that have been completed (including the criminal records check reference number, the date a check was obtained and details of who obtained it). For childminders, the relevant information will be kept by Ofsted or the agency with which the childminder is registered.

3.13. Providers must also meet their responsibilities under the Safeguarding Vulnerable Groups Act 2006, which includes a duty to make a referral to the Disclosure and Barring Service where a member of staff is dismissed (or would have been, had the person not left the setting first) because they have harmed a child or put a child at risk of harm[25].

Disqualification

3.14. A provider or a childcare worker may be disqualified from registration[26]. In the event of the disqualification of a provider, the provider must not continue as an early years provider – nor be directly concerned in the management of such provision. Where a person is disqualified, the provider must not employ that person in connection with early years provision. Where an employer becomes aware of relevant information that may lead to disqualification of an employee, the provider must take appropriate action to ensure the safety of children.

3.15. A provider or a childcare worker may also be disqualified because they live in the same household as another person who is disqualified, or because they live in the same household where a disqualified person is employed. If a provider or

---

[23] Except convictions or cautions that are protected for the purposes of the Rehabilitation of Offenders Act 1974.

[24] DBS disclosures and barred list information are only issued to the potential employee; providers must check the disclosure and consider whether it contains any information that would suggest the person was unsuitable for the position, before an individual starts work with children. Where a potential or existing employee has subscribed to the online DBS Update service, providers should check the status of the disclosure. Where the check identifies there has been a change to the disclosure details, a new enhanced DBS disclosure must be applied for. Before accessing the DBS update service consent to do so must be obtained from the member of staff.

[25] Section 35 of the Safeguarding Vulnerable Groups Act 2006.

[26] In accordance with regulations made under Section 75 of the Childcare Act 2006. Schools are required to have regard to the disqualification guidance published by the Department for Education, which is available at: www.gov.uk/government/publications/disqualification-under-the-childcare-act-2006. Other providers may also find it helpful to refer to this guidance. The Department for Education is considering making changes to the Childcare (Disqualification) Regulations 2009 following a consultation from 6 May to 1 July 2016. The consultation is available at: www.gov.uk/government/consultations/childcare-workers-changes-to-disqualification-arrangements.

childcare worker is disqualified they may, in some circumstances, be able to obtain a 'waiver' from Ofsted.

3.16. A registered provider must notify Ofsted or the agency with which the childminder is registered of any significant event which is likely to affect the suitability of any person who is in regular contact with children on the premises where childcare is provided. The disqualification of an employee could be an instance of a significant event.

3.17. The registered provider must give Ofsted or the childminder agency with which they are registered, the following information about themselves or about any person who lives in the same household as the registered provider or who is employed in the household:

- details of any order, determination, conviction, or other ground for disqualification from registration under regulations made under section 75 of the Childcare Act 2006

- the date of the order, determination or conviction, or the date when the other ground for disqualification arose

- the body or court which made the order, determination or conviction, and the sentence (if any) imposed

- a certified copy of the relevant order (in relation to an order or conviction)

3.18. The information must be provided to Ofsted or the childminder agency with which they are registered as soon as reasonably practicable, but at the latest within 14 days of the date the provider became aware of the information or ought reasonably to have become aware of it if they had made reasonable enquiries[27].

Staff taking medication/other substances

3.19. Practitioners must not be under the influence of alcohol or any other substance which may affect their ability to care for children. If practitioners are taking medication which may affect their ability to care for children, those practitioners should seek medical advice. Providers must ensure that those practitioners only work directly with children if medical advice confirms that the medication is unlikely to impair that staff member's ability to look after children properly. Staff medication on the premises must be securely stored, and out of reach of children, at all times.

---

[27] This requirement is set out in Regulation 12 of the Childcare (Disqualification) Regulations 2009 (S.I. 2009/1547).

Staff qualifications, training, support and skills

3.20. The daily experience of children in early years settings and the overall quality of provision depends on all practitioners having appropriate qualifications, training, skills and knowledge and a clear understanding of their roles and responsibilities. Providers must ensure that all staff receive induction training to help them understand their roles and responsibilities. Induction training must include information about emergency evacuation procedures, safeguarding, child protection, and health and safety issues. Providers must support staff to undertake appropriate training and professional development opportunities to ensure they offer quality learning and development experiences for children that continually improves.

3.21. Providers must put appropriate arrangements in place for the supervision of staff who have contact with children and families. Effective supervision provides support, coaching and training for the practitioner and promotes the interests of children. Supervision should foster a culture of mutual support, teamwork and continuous improvement, which encourages the confidential discussion of sensitive issues.

3.22. Supervision should provide opportunities for staff to:

- discuss any issues – particularly concerning children's development or well-being, including child protection concerns

- identify solutions to address issues as they arise

- receive coaching to improve their personal effectiveness

3.23. In group settings, the manager must hold at least a full and relevant[28] level 3[29] qualification and at least half of all other staff must hold at least a full and relevant level 2 qualification. The manager should have at least two years' experience of working in an early years setting, or have at least two years' other suitable experience. The provider must ensure there is a named deputy who, in their judgement, is capable and qualified to take charge in the manager's absence.

3.24. Childminders must have completed training which helps them to understand and implement the EYFS before they can register with Ofsted or a childminder agency. Childminders are accountable for the quality of the work of any assistants, and must be satisfied that assistants are competent in the areas of work they undertake.

---

[28] As defined by the Department for Education on the Early Years Qualifications List published on GOV.UK, which also includes information on equivalent overseas qualifications.
[29] To count in the ratios at level 3, staff holding an Early Years Educator qualification must also have achieved a suitable level 2 qualification in English and maths as defined by the Department for Education on the Early Years Qualifications List published on GOV.UK.

3.25. At least one person who has a current paediatric first aid (PFA) certificate must be on the premises and available at all times when children are present, and must accompany children on outings. The certificate must be for a full course consistent with the criteria set out in Annex A. Childminders, and any assistant who might be in sole charge of the children for any period of time, must hold a full current PFA certificate. PFA training[30] must be renewed every three years and be relevant for workers caring for young children and where relevant, babies. Providers should take into account the number of children, staff and layout of premises to ensure that a paediatric first aider is able to respond to emergencies quickly. All newly qualified[31] entrants to the early years workforce who have completed a level 2 and/or level 3 qualification on or after 30 June 2016, must also have either a full PFA or an emergency PFA certificate within three months of starting work[32] in order to be included in the required staff:child ratios at level 2 or level 3 in an early years setting[33]. Providers should display (or make available to parents) staff PFA certificates or a list of staff who have a current PFA certificate.

3.26. Providers must ensure that staff have sufficient understanding and use of English to ensure the well-being of children in their care. For example, settings must be in a position to keep records in English, to liaise with other agencies in English, to summon emergency help, and to understand instructions such as those for the safety of medicines or food hygiene.

Key person

3.27. Each child must be assigned a key person. Their role is to help ensure that every child's care is tailored to meet their individual needs (in accordance with

---

[30] Providers are responsible for identifying and selecting a competent training provider to deliver their PFA training. Training is available from a wide range of providers including: those who offer regulated qualifications; or the Voluntary Aid Societies (St John Ambulance, the British Red Cross and St Andrew's First Aid who together are acknowledged by the Health and Safety Executive (HSE) as one of the standard-setters for currently accepted first aid practice for first aid at work training courses); or those who operate under voluntary accreditation schemes; or one that is a member of a trade body with an approval and monitoring scheme; or those who operate independently of any such accreditation scheme. The Register of Regulated Qualifications may help providers identify PFA providers, which can be found at: http://register.ofqual.gov.uk/qualification. It may also be helpful to refer to HSE's guidance about choosing a first aid training provider, which can be found at: www.hse.gov.uk/pubns/geis3.htm

[31] In this context, "newly qualified entrants" includes staff who have been apprentices or long term students who have gained a level 2 or level 3 early years qualification.[32] Newly qualified entrants who started work between 30 June 2016 and 2 April 2017 must have either a full PFA or an emergency PFA certificate by 2 July 2017 in order to be included in the required staff:child ratios at level 2 or level 3 in an early years setting.

[32] Newly qualified entrants who started work between 30 June 2016 and 2 April 2017 must have either a full PFA or an emergency PFA certificate by 2 July 2017 in order to be included in the required staff:child ratios at level 2 or level 3 in an early years setting.

[33] Providers can make an exception to this requirement where a newly qualified entrant to the workforce is unable to gain a PFA certificate if a disability would prevent them from doing so. Such a newly qualified entrant can still be included in the staff:child ratios if otherwise competent to carry out their childcare duties. Where possible, such staff should attend a relevant PFA training course and obtain written evidence of attendance.

paragraph 1.10), to help the child become familiar with the setting, offer a settled relationship for the child and build a relationship with their parents.

Staff:child ratios – all providers (including childminders)

3.28. Staffing arrangements must meet the needs of all children and ensure their safety. Providers must ensure that children are adequately supervised and decide how to deploy staff to ensure children's needs are met. Providers must inform parents and/or carers about staff deployment, and, when relevant and practical, aim to involve them in these decisions. Children must usually be within sight and hearing of staff and always within sight or hearing.

3.29. Only those aged 17 or over may be included in ratios (and staff under 17 should be supervised at all times). Students on long term placements and volunteers (aged 17 or over) and staff working as apprentices in early education (aged 16 or over) may be included in the ratios if the provider is satisfied that they are competent and responsible.

3.30. The ratio and qualification requirements below apply to the total number of staff available to work directly with children[34]. Exceptionally, and where the quality of care and safety and security of children is maintained, changes to the ratios may be made. For group settings providing overnight care, the relevant ratios continue to apply and at least one member of staff must be awake at all times.

Early years providers (other than childminders)

3.31. For children aged under two:

- there must be at least one member of staff for every three children

- at least one member of staff must hold a full and relevant level 3 qualification, and must be suitably experienced in working with children under two

- at least half of all other staff must hold a full and relevant level 2 qualification

- at least half of all staff must have received training that specifically addresses the care of babies

- where there is an under two-year-olds' room, the member of staff in charge of that room must, in the judgement of the provider, have suitable experience of working with under twos

3.32. For children aged two:

---

[34] Ofsted may determine that providers must observe a higher staff:child ratio than outlined here to ensure the safety and welfare of children.

- there must be at least one member of staff for every four children[35]

- at least one member of staff must hold a full and relevant level 3 qualification

- at least half of all other staff must hold a full and relevant level 2 qualification

3.33. For children aged three and over in registered early years provision where a person with Qualified Teacher Status, Early Years Professional Status, Early Years Teacher Status or another suitable level 6 qualification is working directly with the children[36]:

- there must be at least one member of staff for every 13 children

- at least one other member of staff must hold a full and relevant level 3 qualification

3.34. For children aged three and over at any time in registered early years provision when a person with Qualified Teacher Status, Early Years Professional Status, Early Years Teacher Status or another suitable level 6 qualification is not working directly with the children:

- there must be at least one member of staff for every eight children

- at least one member of staff must hold a full and relevant level 3 qualification

- at least half of all other staff must hold a full and relevant level 2 qualification

3.35. For children aged three and over in independent schools (including in nursery classes in free schools and academies), where a person with Qualified Teacher Status, Early Years Professional Status, Early Years Teacher Status or another suitable level 6 qualification, an instructor[37], or another suitably qualified overseas trained teacher, is working directly with the children:

- for classes where the majority of children will reach the age of five or older within the school year, there must be at least one member of staff for every 30 children[38]

---

[35] In a maintained school or non-maintained special school, where the two-year-olds are pupils, staff must additionally be under the direction and supervision of a qualified or nominated teacher when carrying out specified work (as laid out in the Education (Specified Work) (England) Regulations 2012). Specified work broadly encompasses lesson (or curriculum) planning, delivering lessons, assessing the development, progress and attainment of pupils and reporting on the latter. The headteacher must be satisfied that the staff have the skills, expertise and experience needed to carry out the work and determine the appropriate level of direction and supervision.

[36] We expect the teacher (or equivalent) to be working with children for the vast majority of the time. Where they need to be absent for short periods of time, the provider will need to ensure that quality and safety is maintained.

[37] An instructor is a person at the school who provides education which consists of instruction in any art or skill, or in any subject or group of subjects, in circumstances where: (a) special qualifications or experience or both are required for such instruction; and (b) the person or body of persons responsible for the management of the school is satisfied as to the qualifications or experience (or both) of the person providing education.

[38] Subject to any permitted exceptions under The Schools Admissions (Infant Class Sizes) Regulations 2012 S.I. 2012/10.

- for all other classes there must be at least one member of staff for every 13 children

- at least one other member of staff must hold a full and relevant level 3 qualification

3.36. For children aged three and over in independent schools (including in nursery classes in academies), where there is no person with Qualified Teacher Status, Early Years Professional Status, Early Years Teacher Status or another suitable level 6 qualification, no instructor, and no suitably qualified overseas trained teacher, working directly with the children:

- there must be at least one member of staff for every eight children

- at least one member of staff must hold a full and relevant level 3 qualification

- at least half of all other staff must hold a full and relevant level 2 qualification

3.37. For children aged three and over in maintained nursery schools and nursery classes in maintained schools[39]:

- there must be at least one member of staff for every 13 children[40]

- at least one member of staff must be a school teacher as defined by section 122 of the Education Act 2002[41]

- at least one other member of staff must hold a full and relevant level 3 qualification[42]

3.38. Reception classes in maintained schools and academies are subject to infant class size legislation.[43] The School Admissions (Infant Class Size) Regulations 2012 limit the size of infant classes to 30 pupils per school teacher[44] (subject to permitted exceptions) while an ordinary teaching session is conducted. 'School teachers' do not include teaching assistants, higher level teaching assistants or other support staff. Consequently, in an ordinary teaching session, a school must

[39] Where schools have provision run by the governing body (under section 27 of the Education Act 2002) for three- and four-year-olds who are not pupils of the school, they can apply: a 1:13 ratio where a person with a suitable level 6 qualification is working directly with the children (as in paragraph 3.33); or a 1:8 ratio where a person with a suitable level 6 qualification is not working directly with children but at least one member of staff present holds a level 3 qualification (as in paragraph 3.34).

[40] Where children in nursery classes attend school for longer than the school day or in the school holidays, in provision run directly by the governing body or the proprietor, with no teacher present, a ratio of one member of staff to every eight children can be applied if at least one member of staff holds a full and relevant level 3 qualification, and at least half of all other staff hold a full and relevant level 2 qualification.

[41] See also the Education (School Teachers' Prescribed Qualifications, etc) Order 2003 and the Education (School Teachers' Qualifications) (England) Regulations 2003.

[42] Provided that the person meets all relevant staff qualification requirement as required by The School Staffing (England) Regulations 2009.

[43] Academies are required by their funding agreements to comply with the School Admissions Code and the law relating to admissions although the Secretary of State has the power to vary this requirement where there is demonstratable need.

[44] As defined by section 122 of the Education Act 2002.

employ sufficient school teachers to enable it to teach its infant classes in groups of no more than 30 per school teacher[45].

3.39. Some schools may choose to mix their reception classes with groups of younger children (nursery pupils, non pupils or younger children from a registered provider), in which case they must determine ratios within mixed groups, guided by all relevant ratio requirements and by the needs of individual children within the group. In exercising this discretion, the school must comply with the statutory requirements relating to the education of children of compulsory school age and infant class sizes. Schools' partner providers must meet the relevant ratio requirements for their provision.

Before/after school care and holiday provision

3.40. Where the provision is solely before/after school care or holiday provision for children who normally attend Reception class (or older) during the school day, there must be sufficient staff as for a class of 30 children. It is for providers to determine how many staff are needed to ensure the safety and welfare of children, bearing in mind the type(s) of activity and the age and needs of the children. It is also for providers to determine what qualifications, if any, the manager and/or staff should have. See footnote 5 at paragraph 1.1 for the learning and development requirements for providers offering care exclusively before/after school or during the school holidays.

Childminders

3.41. At any one time, childminders (whether providing the childminding on domestic or non-domestic premises) may care for a maximum of six children under the age of eight[46]. Of these six children, a maximum of three may be young children, and there should only be one child under the age of one. A child is a young child up until 1st September following his or her fifth birthday. Any care provided for older children must not adversely affect the care of children receiving early years provision.

3.42. If a childminder can demonstrate to parents and/or carers and Ofsted inspectors or their childminder agency that the individual needs of all the children are being met, exceptions to the usual ratios can be made, for example, when childminders are caring for sibling babies, or when caring for their own baby, or to maintain continuity of care. If children aged four and five only attend the childminding setting before and/or after a normal school day, and/or during school holidays,

---

[45] The Specified Work Regulations 2012 allow a non-teacher to carry out the work of the teacher ("specified work") where the non-teacher is assisting or supporting the work of the teacher, is subject to the teacher's direction and supervision as arranged with the headteacher, and the headteacher is satisfied that that person has the skills, expertise and experience required to carry out the specified work.
[46] Including the childminder's own children or any other children for whom they are responsible such as those being fostered.

they may be cared for at the same time as three other young children. But in all circumstances, the total number of children under the age of eight being cared for must not exceed six.

3.43. If a childminder employs an assistant or works with another childminder, each childminder (or assistant) may care for the number of children permitted by the ratios specified above[47]. Children may be left in the sole care of childminders' assistants for two hours at most in a single day[48]. Childminders must obtain parents and/or carers' permission to leave children with an assistant, including for very short periods of time. For childminders providing overnight care, the ratios continue to apply and the childminder must always be able to hear the children (this may be via a monitor).

Health

Medicines

3.44. The provider must promote the good health of children attending the setting. They must have a procedure, discussed with parents and/or carers, for responding to children who are ill or infectious, take necessary steps to prevent the spread of infection, and take appropriate action if children are ill[49].

3.45. Providers must have and implement a policy, and procedures, for administering medicines. It must include systems for obtaining information about a child's needs for medicines, and for keeping this information up-to-date. Training must be provided for staff where the administration of medicine requires medical or technical knowledge. Prescription medicines must not be administered unless they have been prescribed for a child by a doctor, dentist, nurse or pharmacist (medicines containing aspirin should only be given if prescribed by a doctor).

3.46. Medicine (both prescription and non-prescription) must only be administered to a child where written permission for that particular medicine has been obtained from the child's parent and/or carer. Providers must keep a written record each time a medicine is administered to a child, and inform the child's parents and/or carers on the same day, or as soon as reasonably practicable.

---

[47] Subject to any restrictions imposed by Ofsted or the relevant childminder agency on registration.
[48] The Childcare (Exemptions from Registration) Order 2008 specifies that where provision is made for a particular child for two hours or less a day, the carer is exempt from registration as a childminder.
[49] Guidance on Infection Control in Schools and other Childcare Settings which sets out when and for how long children need to be excluded from settings, when treatment/medication is required and where to get further advice can be found at: www.gov.uk/government/publications/infection-control-in-schools-poster#history

Food and drink

3.47. Where children are provided with meals, snacks and drinks, they must be healthy, balanced and nutritious. Before a child is admitted to the setting the provider must also obtain information about any special dietary requirements, preferences and food allergies that the child has, and any special health requirements. Fresh drinking water must be available and accessible at all times. Providers must record and act on information from parents and carers about a child's dietary needs.

3.48. There must be an area which is adequately equipped to provide healthy meals, snacks and drinks for children as necessary. There must be suitable facilities for the hygienic preparation of food for children, if necessary including suitable sterilisation equipment for babies' food. Providers must be confident that those responsible for preparing and handling food are competent to do so. In group provision, all staff involved in preparing and handling food must receive training in food hygiene.

3.49. Registered providers must notify Ofsted or the childminder agency with which they are registered of any food poisoning affecting two or more children cared for on the premises. Notification must be made as soon as is reasonably practicable, but in any event within 14 days of the incident. A registered provider, who, without reasonable excuse, fails to comply with this requirement, commits an offence.

Accident or injury

3.50. Providers must ensure there is a first aid box accessible at all times with appropriate content for use with children. Providers must keep a written record of accidents or injuries and first aid treatment. Providers must inform parents and/or carers of any accident or injury sustained by the child on the same day as, or as soon as reasonably practicable after, and of any first aid treatment given.

3.51. Registered providers must notify Ofsted or the childminder agency with which they are registered of any serious accident, illness or injury to, or death of, any child while in their care, and of the action taken. Notification must be made as soon as is reasonably practicable, but in any event within 14 days of the incident occurring. A registered provider, who, without reasonable excuse, fails to comply with this requirement, commits an offence. Providers must notify local child protection agencies of any serious accident or injury to, or the death of, any child while in their care, and must act on any advice from those agencies.

Managing behaviour

3.52. Providers are responsible for managing children's behaviour in an appropriate way. Providers must not give corporal punishment to a child. Providers must take all reasonable steps to ensure that corporal punishment is not given by any person who cares for or is in regular contact with a child, or by any person living or working in the premises where care is provided. Any early years provider who fails to meet these requirements commits an offence. A person will not be taken to have used corporal punishment (and therefore will not have committed an offence), where physical intervention[50] was taken for the purposes of averting immediate danger of personal injury to any person (including the child) or to manage a child's behaviour if absolutely necessary. Providers, including childminders, must keep a record of any occasion where physical intervention is used, and parents and/or carers must be informed on the same day, or as soon as reasonably practicable.

3.53. Providers must not threaten corporal punishment, and must not use or threaten any punishment which could adversely affect a child's well-being.

Safety and suitability of premises, environment and equipment

Safety

3.54. Providers must ensure that their premises, including overall floor space and outdoor spaces, are fit for purpose and suitable for the age of children cared for and the activities provided on the premises. Providers must comply with requirements of health and safety legislation (including fire safety and hygiene requirements).

3.55. Providers must take reasonable steps to ensure the safety of children, staff and others on the premises in the case of fire or any other emergency, and must have an emergency evacuation procedure. Providers must have appropriate fire detection and control equipment (for example, fire alarms, smoke detectors, fire blankets and/or fire extinguishers) which is in working order. Fire exits must be clearly identifiable, and fire doors must be free of obstruction and easily opened from the inside.

Smoking

3.56. Providers must not allow smoking in or on the premises when children are present or about to be present.

---

[50] Physical intervention is where practitioners use reasonable force to prevent children from injuring themselves or others or damaging property.

Premises

3.57. The premises and equipment must be organised in a way that meets the needs of children. Providers must meet the following indoor space requirements[51]:

- Children under two years: 3.5 m² per child

- Two year olds: 2.5 m² per child

- Children aged three to five years: 2.3 m² per child

3.58. Providers must provide access to an outdoor play area or, if that is not possible, ensure that outdoor activities are planned and taken on a daily basis (unless circumstances make this inappropriate, for example unsafe weather conditions). Providers must follow their legal responsibilities under the Equality Act 2010 (for example, the provisions on reasonable adjustments).

3.59. Sleeping children must be frequently checked. Except in childminding settings, there should be a separate baby room for children under the age of two. However, providers must ensure that children in a baby room have contact with older children and are moved into the older age group when appropriate.

3.60. Providers must ensure there is an adequate number of toilets and hand basins available. Except in childminding settings, there should usually be separate toilet facilities for adults. Providers must ensure there are suitable hygienic changing facilities for changing any children who are in nappies and providers should ensure that an adequate supply of clean bedding, towels, spare clothes and any other necessary items is always available.

3.61. Providers must also ensure that there is an area where staff may talk to parents and/or carers confidentially, as well as an area in group settings for staff to take breaks away from areas being used by children.

3.62. Providers must only release children into the care of individuals who have been notified to the provider by the parent, and must ensure that children do not leave the premises unsupervised. Providers must take all reasonable steps to prevent unauthorised persons entering the premises[52], and have an agreed procedure for checking the identity of visitors. Providers must consider what additional measures are necessary when children stay overnight.

3.63. Providers must carry the appropriate insurance (e.g. public liability insurance) to cover all premises from which they provide childcare or childminding.

---

[51] These calculations should be based on the net or useable areas of the rooms used by the children, not including storage areas, thoroughfares, dedicated staff areas, cloakrooms, utility rooms, kitchens and toilets.

[52] Where childminders are operating out of non-domestic premises which are routinely accessed by members of the public (e.g. a hotel or a community centre), childminders must take all reasonable steps to prevent unauthorised persons entering the part of those premises in which the children are being cared for.

Risk assessment

3.64. Providers must ensure that they take all reasonable steps to ensure staff and children in their care are not exposed to risks and must be able to demonstrate how they are managing risks[53]. Providers must determine where it is helpful to make some written risk assessments in relation to specific issues, to inform staff practice, and to demonstrate how they are managing risks if asked by parents and/or carers or inspectors. Risk assessments should identify aspects of the environment that need to be checked on a regular basis, when and by whom those aspects will be checked, and how the risk will be removed or minimised.

Outings

3.65. Children must be kept safe while on outings. Providers must assess the risks or hazards which may arise for the children, and must identify the steps to be taken to remove, minimise and manage those risks and hazards. The assessment must include consideration of adult to child ratios. The risk assessment does not necessarily need to be in writing; this is for providers to judge.

3.66. Vehicles in which children are being transported, and the driver of those vehicles, must be adequately insured.

Special educational needs

3.67. Providers must have arrangements in place to support children with SEN or disabilities. Maintained schools, maintained nursery schools and all providers who are funded by the local authority to deliver early education places must have regard to the Special Educational Needs Code of Practice[54]. Maintained schools and maintained nursery schools must identify a member of staff to act as Special Educational Needs Co-ordinator (SENCO) and other providers (in group provision) are expected to identify a SENCO. Childminders are encouraged to identify a person to act as a SENCO and childminders who are registered with a childminder agency or who are part of a network may wish to share the role between them.

Information and records

3.68. Providers must maintain records and obtain and share information (with parents and carers, other professionals working with the child, the police, social services and Ofsted or the childminder agency with which they are registered, as appropriate) to ensure the safe and efficient management of the setting, and to

---

[53] Guidance on risk assessments, including where written ones may be required where five or more staff are employed, can be obtained from the Health and Safety Executive.
[54] www.gov.uk/government/publications/send-code-of-practice-0-to-25

help ensure the needs of all children are met. Providers must enable a regular two-way flow of information with parents and/or carers, and between providers, if a child is attending more than one setting. If requested, providers should incorporate parents' and/or carers' comments into children's records.

3.69. Records must be easily accessible and available (with prior agreement from Ofsted or the childminder agency with which they are registered, these may be kept securely off the premises). Confidential information and records about staff and children must be held securely and only accessible and available to those who have a right or professional need to see them. Providers must be aware of their responsibilities under the Data Protection Act (DPA) 1998 and where relevant the Freedom of Information Act 2000.

3.70. Providers must ensure that all staff understand the need to protect the privacy of the children in their care as well the legal requirements that exist to ensure that information relating to the child is handled in a way that ensures confidentiality. Parents and/or carers must be given access to all records about their child, provided that no relevant exemptions apply to their disclosure under the DPA[55].

3.71. Records relating to individual children must be retained for a reasonable period of time after they have left the provision [56].

Information about the child

3.72. Providers must record the following information for each child in their care: full name; date of birth; name and address of every parent and/or carer who is known to the provider (and information about any other person who has parental responsibility for the child); which parent(s) and/or carer(s) the child normally lives with; and emergency contact details for parents and/or carers.

Information for parents and carers

3.73. Providers must make the following information available to parents and/or carers:

- how the EYFS is being delivered in the setting, and how parents and/or carers can access more information

---

[55] The Data Protection Act 1998 (DPA) gives parents and carers the right to access information about their child that a provider holds. However, the DPA also sets out specific exemptions under which certain personal information may, under specific circumstances, be withheld from release. For example, a relevant professional will need to give careful consideration as to whether the disclosure of certain information about a child could cause harm either to the child or any other individual. It is therefore essential that all providers/staff in early years settings have an understanding of how data protection laws operate. Further guidance can be found on the website of the Information Commissioner's Office at: www.ico.gov.uk/for_organisations/data_protection.aspx

[56] Individual providers should determine how long to retain records relating to individual children.

- the range and type of activities and experiences provided for children, the daily routines of the setting, and how parents and carers can share learning at home

- how the setting supports children with special educational needs and disabilities

- food and drinks provided for children

- details of the provider's policies and procedures (all providers except childminders (see paragraph 3.3) must make copies available on request) including the procedure to be followed in the event of a parent and/or carer failing to collect a child at the appointed time, or in the event of a child going missing at, or away from, the setting

- staffing in the setting; the name of their child's key person and their role; and a telephone number for parents and/or carers to contact in an emergency

Complaints

3.74. Providers must put in place a written procedure for dealing with concerns and complaints from parents and/or carers, and must keep a written record of any complaints, and their outcome. Childminders are not required to have a written procedure for handling complaints, but they must keep a record of any complaints they receive and their outcome. All providers must investigate written complaints relating to their fulfilment of the EYFS requirements and notify complainants of the outcome of the investigation within 28 days of having received the complaint. The record of complaints must be made available to Ofsted or the relevant childminder agency on request.

3.75. Providers must make available to parents and/or carers details about how to contact Ofsted or the childminder agency with which the provider is registered as appropriate, if they believe the provider is not meeting the EYFS requirements. If providers become aware that they are to be inspected by Ofsted or have a quality assurance visit by the childminder agency, they must notify parents and/or carers. After an inspection by Ofsted or a quality assurance visit by their childminder agency, providers must supply a copy of the report to parents and/or carers of children attending on a regular basis.

Information about the provider

3.76. Providers must hold the following documentation:

- name, home address and telephone number of the provider and any other person living or employed on the premises (this requirement does not apply to childminders)

- name, home address and telephone number of anyone else who will regularly be in unsupervised contact with the children attending the early years provision

- a daily record of the names of the children being cared for on the premises, their hours of attendance and the names of each child's key person

- their certificate of registration (which must be displayed at the setting and shown to parents and/or carers on request)

Changes that must be notified to Ofsted or the relevant childminder agency (CMA)

3.77. All registered early years providers must notify Ofsted or the CMA with which they are registered of any change:

- in the address of the premises (and seek approval to operate from those premises where appropriate); to the premises which may affect the space available to children and the quality of childcare available to them; in the name or address of the provider, or the provider's other contact information; to the person who is managing the early years provision; in the persons aged 16 years or older living or working on any domestic premises from which childminding is provided; or to the persons caring for children on any premises where childminding is provided[57]

- any proposal to change the hours during which childcare is provided; or to provide overnight care

- any significant event which is likely to affect the suitability of the early years provider or any person who cares for, or is in regular contact with, children on the premises to look after children

- where the early years provision is provided by a company, any change in the name or registered number of the company

- where the early years provision is provided by a charity, any change in the name or registration number of the charity

- where the childcare is provided by a partnership, body corporate or unincorporated association, any change to the 'nominated individual'

- where the childcare is provided by a partnership, body corporate or unincorporated association whose sole or main purpose is the provision of childcare, any change to the individuals who are partners in, or a director, secretary or other officer or members of its governing body

---

[57] A person is not considered to be working on the premises if none of their work is done in the part of the premises in which children are cared for, or if they do not work on the premises at times when children are there.

3.78. Where providers are required to notify Ofsted or their CMA about a change of person except for managers, as specified in paragraph 3.77 above, providers must give Ofsted or their CMA the new person's name, any former names or aliases, date of birth, and home address. If there is a change of manager, providers must notify Ofsted or their CMA that a new manager has been appointed. Where it is reasonably practicable to do so, notification must be made in advance. In other cases, notification must be made as soon as is reasonably practicable, but always within 14 days. A registered provider who, without reasonable excuse, fails to comply with these requirements commits an offence.

Annex A: Criteria for effective PFA training

1. Training is designed for workers caring for young children in the absence of their parents and is appropriate to the age of the children being cared for.

2. Following training an assessment of competence leads to the award of a certificate.

3. The certificate must be renewed every three years.

4. Adequate resuscitation and other equipment including baby and junior models must be provided, so that all trainees are able to practice and demonstrate techniques.

5. The **emergency PFA** course should be undertaken face-to-face and last for a minimum of 6 hours (excluding breaks) and cover the following areas:

   - Be able to assess an emergency situation and prioritise what action to take
   - Help a baby or child who is unresponsive and breathing normally
   - Help a baby or child who is unresponsive and not breathing normally
   - Help a baby or child who is having a seizure
   - Help a baby or child who is choking
   - Help a baby or child who is bleeding
   - Help a baby or child who is suffering from shock caused by severe blood loss (hypovolemic shock)

6. The **full PFA** course should last for a minimum of 12 hours (excluding breaks) and cover the areas set out in paragraph 5 as well as the following areas:

   - Help a baby or child who is suffering from anaphylactic shock
   - Help a baby or child who has had an electric shock
   - Help a baby or child who has burns or scalds
   - Help a baby or child who has a suspected fracture
   - Help a baby or child with head, neck or back injuries
   - Help a baby or child who is suspected of being poisoned
   - Help a baby or child with a foreign body in eyes, ears or nose
   - Help a baby or child with an eye injury
   - Help a baby or child with a bite or sting
   - Help a baby or child who is suffering from the effects of extreme heat or cold
   - Help a baby or child having: a diabetic emergency; an asthma attack; an allergic reaction; meningitis; and/or febrile convulsions
   - Understand the role and responsibilities of the paediatric first aider (including appropriate contents of a first aid box and the need for recording accidents and incidents)

7. Providers should consider whether paediatric first aiders need to undertake annual refresher training, during any three year certification period to help maintain basic skills and keep up to date with any changes to PFA procedures.

Department
for Education

 Follow us on Twitter:
@educationgovuk

 Like us on Facebook:
facebook.com/educationgovuk

Printed in Great Britain
by Amazon

85969094R00023